Contents

Introduction and Things you will need 4

Words of advice.. 6

First steps – making the slip loop 8

How to hold the work – ready for chain 10

Making the chain 12

First row of double crochet 14

Next row of double crochet 16

A purse 18

Handkerchief case 20

Square ball for baby 22

Maxi-dress for dolly 24

Tension 26

Tie for young brother 28

Treble stitches 30

Scarf made from trebles 34

Cap to match scarf 36

Half-treble stitches 38

Slip stitch 40

Practice in trebles, half-trebles
  and slip-stitches – a belt 42

Rounds and squares 44

A little mat 46

Making a square ..

A dolly's poncho ..

D1327929

Crochet

by WYNNE BROUGHTON

with illustrations by ERIC WINTER

Ladybird Books Ltd Loughborough

Introduction

CROCHET is really quite easy to learn. As in any handicraft, there are just a few simple rules to follow during practice.

If every page and picture is studied carefully, you will soon find that you can make all the things in the book, for yourself or as presents for your family and friends.

Later on you will be able to work more difficult patterns, or even think up some new ones by yourself.

For your crochet work you will need:

A crochet hook size 5.00.

Several little balls of brightly coloured double crêpe (or similar thickness) wool, for practice.

A small pair of sharp scissors to cut the wool.

A blunt-ended wool needle with a big eye, for sewing up your work.

A ruler, or tape measure, marked in centimetres.

A workbag, or box, to keep everything together, neatly and tidily.

0 7214 0406 5

A few words of advice:

Always remember:

1. Wash your hands and dry them well before crochet work begins.

2. Keep your fingers, hands and wrists quite relaxed, never stiff.

3. Reverse the instructions if you are LEFT HANDED. That is, where the directions say RIGHT hand, use your LEFT, and where they say LEFT, use your RIGHT. If you prop up this book and place a small mirror opposite each picture the difference will be easier to follow.

4. Keep the hooked-end facing you as you work. Never twiddle the hook around as you make a stitch.

5. Form the habit of counting the stitches in every row. It is so easy to miss one, especially the last stitch.

6. Learn the shortened terms in crochet, called *abbreviations*, as you work through these pages. You will find a list of them on the inside back cover. Later on in the book, they are shown in brackets (. . .) against the full word.

First steps

Crochet begins with a slip loop which can be moved easily along the stem of the hook.

To make the slip loop

1.   In the left hand, take the end of a ball of wool and form it into a ring. Hold the ring between your thumb and first finger, and drop the part leading to the ball down the back of the ring as shown (Picture 1).

2.   Take the crochet hook in the other hand, holding it as you would a pencil, between thumb and first finger and at the flattened part of the stem (Picture 2).

3.   Put the hooked end right under the middle thread in the ring, catching the wool in the hooked end (Picture 3).

4.   Now, keeping the loop on the hook, pull this middle thread through until the loop closes over the stem and slips easily along (Picture 4).

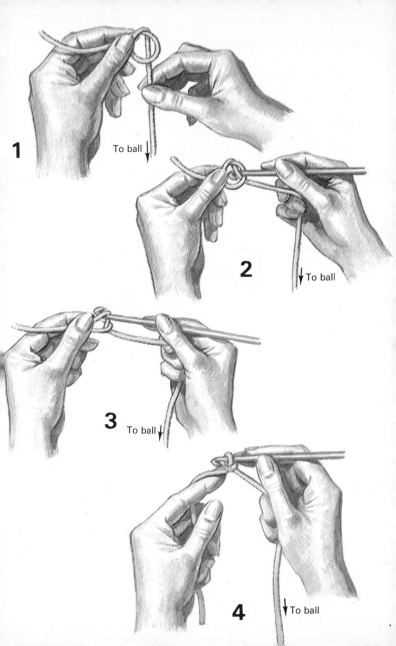

1 To ball↓

2 ↓To ball

3 To ball↓

4 ↓To ball

How to hold your work

1. The slip knot is now safely on the crochet hook. In the LEFT hand (or RIGHT if you are left-handed) hold the slip loop *knot* just underneath the hook, between your thumb and first finger (Picture 1).

2. From the slip loop, take the wool that leads to the ball over the first two fingers of the same hand, then under the third finger, and then right round the little finger (Picture 2).

3. Now hold the crochet hook in your RIGHT hand (or LEFT if you are left-handed), holding the crochet hook between your thumb and first finger at the flattened part of the stem. Rest your second finger on the hook, just in front of your first. Make sure the hooked end is always facing you and pointing slightly downwards (Picture 3).

4. Raise your second finger a little with the wool still going over it, so that the hooked end will be able to catch up the wool that is between your first and second fingers. Both hands, hook and wool are shown in working position in Picture 4.

You are now ready to make your first chain stitches, called *the foundation chain*, from which most crochet work grows.

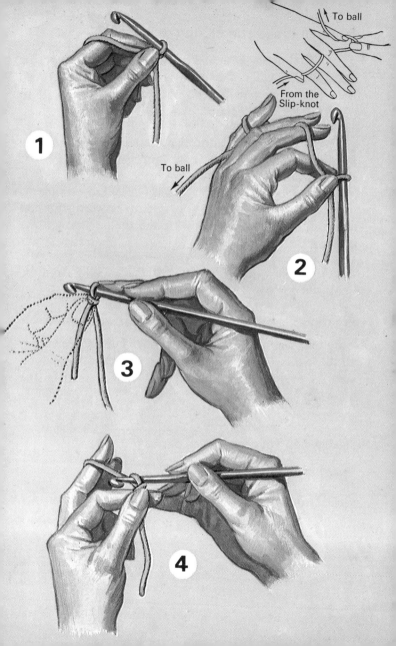

To ball

From the
Slip-knot

To ball

1

2

3

4

How to make the chain (ch.)

1. Holding the knot and hook as in Picture 1 opposite, take the hook end under and over the wool that is between the first and second fingers, until it is in position 2. In patterns this is called *yarn over hook* (y.o.h.).

2. Draw this thread through the loop on the hook to position 3. You have just made your first chain stitch.

3. Make 10 more chain stitches (ch.sts.), by taking the hook every time under the wool (y.o.h.) between your first and second fingers and drawing the thread through the loop on the hook.

You will now have 11 chain stitches hanging from the hook (Picture 4).

Practice

Pull the chain and slip loop undone, and keep repeating all the movements from the beginning of page 8 until you have 11 evenly formed chain stitches hanging from the hook.

Now you are ready to make 10 double crochet (d.c.) stitches into your foundation chain.

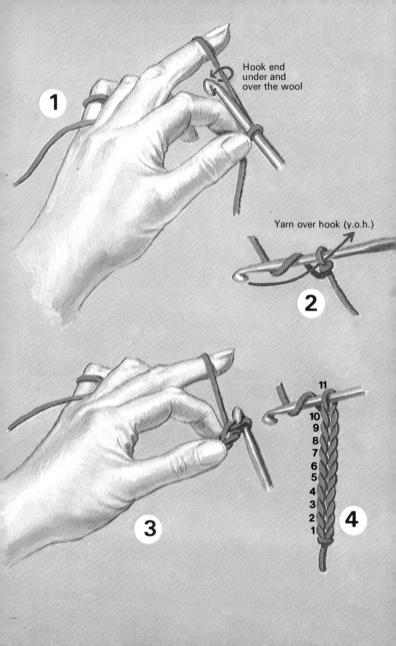

1

Hook end under and over the wool

2

Yarn over hook (y.o.h.)

3

4

11
10
9
8
7
6
5
4
3
2
1

Double crochet (d.c.) stitches

Look closely at your 11 chain stitches. You will notice that each chain stitch has three threads (Picture 1).

Double crochet stitches are made by putting the hook through the top two threads (Picture 1).

1.   Hold the length of chain between thumb and first finger just below the loop on the hook. With the hook in the other hand, put the hook from the front under the two top threads of the *second* chain from the hook (Picture 1).

2.   Now y.o.h. as you did for the chains (Picture 2), and draw this through the two chain threads on the hook. You now have two loops on the hook (Picture 3).

3.   Y.o.h. again, and draw this through both loops on the hook. You now have one loop on the hook, and have made your first double crochet (d.c.) stitch (Picture 4).

4.   For your next double crochet stitch, take the hook from the front under the two top threads of the *next* chain stitch, y.o.h. as before, and draw this through the two threads just taken into the hook.

5.   Y.o.h. again, and draw this through both loops on the hook. Your second double crochet stitch is made.

6.   Repeat **4** and **5**, making one double crochet stitch into every chain stitch to the end of the chain.

7.   Now count the number of chain stitches at the top of the double crochet row just made. There should be 10 double crochet (d.c.) stitches (sts.).

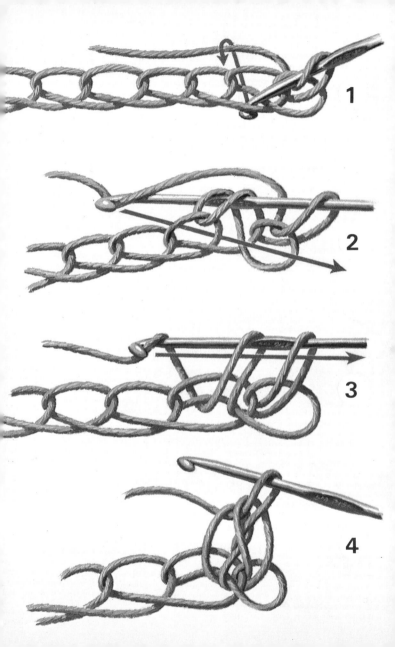

1

2

3

4

To make the next row of double crochet (d.c.) stitches (sts.)

You now have a neat row of double crochet stitches made over the foundation chain.

Turn your work round so that the last double crochet stitch (d.c. st.) is ready for the first st. of the new row.

To make the next row:

1. First make 1 chain (ch.). This is not a stitch, but you will then be ready to begin the row (Picture 1).

2. Take the hook under the two top chain threads of the very first stitch.

3. Take the wool into the hook (y.o.h.) as before, and draw this through the two threads just picked up.

4. Take y.o.h. again, and draw this through both loops on the hook.

Your first d.c. st. of the second row is now made (Picture 2).

5. For the next d.c. st. take the hook under the next two top chain threads of the last row, y.o.h. as before and draw this through both loop threads just picked up, y.o.h. again, and draw through both loops on the hook.

Your next d.c. st. is now made.

6. Repeat (rep.) **5** to the end of the row.

You now have 10 very neatly made d.c. sts. on top of the first row (Picture 3).

Before we learn another stitch, let us make some things in d.c.

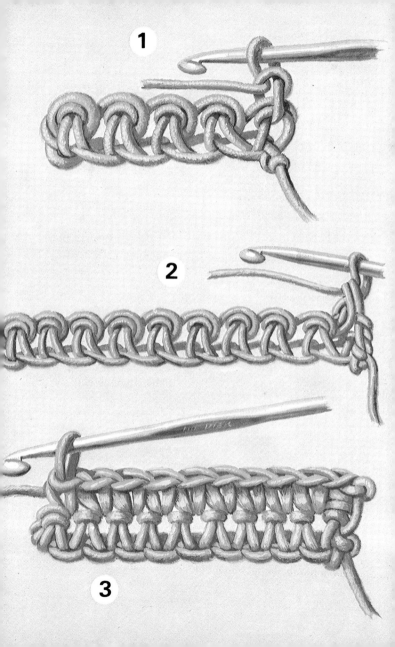

A purse

Before you begin to make the purse, make sure that:

1. You can work double crochet (d.c.) stitches (sts.) evenly and firmly.

2. You know all the abbreviations and signs (see inside back cover) as they will be used in some of the patterns.

An oddment of double crêpe (or similar) wool
A crochet hook size 5.00
A small button
A blunt-ended wool needle for sewing up

Measurement: 11 cm. wide by 6 cm. deep when made up.

To make:

Begin with 25 ch.

1st row: 1 d.c. into 2nd ch. from hook, 1 d.c. into each ch. to end, 1 ch., turn work ready for next row (24 d.c. in all).

2nd row: 1 d.c. into each d.c. of last row (24 d.c.), 1 ch., turn.

3rd to 21st rows: repeat 2nd row, leaving out the 1 ch. at end of 21st row. To finish off, break off the wool, slip the loop off the hook and draw the end of the wool through it.

To make up:

Lay the work flat with the shorter sides at top and bottom. Now fold **A** to **C** and **B** to **D**, leaving 3 cm. from **C** to **E** and **D** to **F** for flap. Neatly oversew the sides together. Fasten off all ends by sewing them in neatly. Sew button about 1 cm. down from middle of underside below flap. To fasten, push button through stitches in middle of flap.

Handkerchief case

An oddment of double crêpe (or similar) wool (about half a ball) in each of 2 colours
About 10 metres of a third colour wool for edging
A crochet hook size 5.00   A wool needle

To make:

Following the directions for the purse on page 18, work 2 pieces, each of 30 rows (one colour for each piece).

To make up:

Pin pieces together along 3 sides, matching the corners.

To join the 3rd colour for edging, put hook through one side stitch of the top piece, about 1 cm. from any corner, and then through the same stitch on the piece underneath. Now place wool into the hook, about 10 cm. from the end of the wool, and draw this through the stitches already on the hook, take the wool double into the hook again, and draw through loop on hook; (1 ch. made which will stand for first d.c.). Now make 3 more ch. and 1 d.c. into same stitches as first ch., (this makes the 1st mini-shell for the edging).

*Now, about 1 cm. from this shell, make another one by putting hook through 1 st. of top and 1 st. of bottom piece, y.o.h., and draw through sts. just picked up, y.o.h. and draw through both loops (1 d.c. made), 3 ch., 1 d.c. into same place as first d.c. (another mini-shell made). Rep. from * along three sides of the case, being sure to work one at each corner. Make more mini-shells along each 4th side separately. Join the last shell to the first with a neat sewing stitch. Fasten off and neatly sew in all ends.

Square ball for baby

It will not roll away, or bounce out of sight!

Oddments of double crêpe (or similar) wool in two colours
A crochet hook size 5.00
A wool needle
For stuffing – strips of soft, clean material or other suitable filling

This ball was worked in two rows of d.c. of first colour and 2 rows of d.c. in second colour, alternately.

NOTE: *To join in the new colour:* At the end of the second row of one colour, when the last 2 loops of the last stitch are on the hook, drop the end of the last colour, take the new colour into the hook about 10 cm. from the end, draw this through the 2 loops on hook; now break off the old colour and very loosely tie the two colours together. Continue with new colour. When each piece is finished, untie all the loose knots, pull them gently to ensure the stitches at the join are even, then sew each end into its own colour on the wrong side.

To make:

Work 2 pieces each of 24 d.c. and 30 rows as for handkerchief case on page 20, working 2 rows alternately in each colour. Fasten off, and sew ends in.

To make up:

Pin together all 4 sides, matching corners. With a neat row of double crochet stitches, join together the first 3 sides. Remove pins from 4th side, and put in the stuffing, pressing it evenly over the inside and into the corners; pin the 4th side together again, and continue to join them with d.c. stitches. Join last d.c. to first d.c. with a sewing stitch. Fasten off and sew in ends.

Maxi-dress for dolly

A doll, measuring about 20 cm. tall

A ball of double crêpe or similar wool (about 20 grams)

A crochet hook size 5.00

About 75 cm. ribbon, 10 mm. wide

A wool needle for sewing up

The skirt   Work 1 piece of 24 d.c. and 30 rows as for purse on page 18.

The bodice   Working *very loosely* make 1 d.c. into the first st. of the row, miss 1 st., 1 d.c. into next st.; continue making 1 d.c. into every other st. to end of row, 1 ch., turn (12 d.c. in all).

Next row: Work 1 d.c. into each of the 12 d.c. of last row, 1 ch., turn.

Next 5 rows: Work 1 d.c. into each d.c. of previous row, 1 ch., turn. On the last row, leave out the 1 ch. at the end.

Break off wool, fasten off, and sew in the ends.

To make up:

Join back seam of skirt with neat oversew stitches. Cut off about 16 cm. of the ribbon and thread through top of bodice; thread the remaining piece of ribbon through waist of dress.

To dress the dolly: Take her arms through top of bodice between the d.c.s of the last row but one; tie a bow in the ribbon at neck and at waist, as in picture.

Tension

Before you do any more crochet, the word *tension* must be explained. This means the number of stitches, or rows, or patterns, it takes to reach a certain measurement.

Printed patterns suggest a certain size of hook to make an article of a certain size. Some people work more loosely or tightly than others and you may have to use a hook of a different size to get the correct result.

Patterns will say something like this:

Tension: Using a No. 5.00 crochet hook, 5 d.c.=3 cm. This means it takes 5 d.c. to give a width of 3 cm.

To find out whether you should work with the hook suggested, or with a larger or smaller size, you work what is called the *tension test piece*, and if this gives the correct measurement then the finished article will be the correct size. This is important if you are to get the correct result.

To make the tension test piece

This should be at least 4 times the size in width and number of rows given under TENSION. For the above piece, you would make 21 ch. and work 4 rows of d.c.

Lay the test piece flat and, taking a ruler or tape measure, place this over the work in the middle of the 2nd or 3rd row of d.c. Place a knob pin at the beginning of a 3 cm. measurement and another at the end, as the picture shows.

Now count the number of d.c. sts. between the pins. If there are just 5, use the No. 5.00 hook. If there are 6, try a size 5.50 hook to make the sts. slightly bigger; if only 4, try a 4.50 hook to make the sts. slightly smaller.

A tie for a young brother

1 25-gram ball of double crêpe (or similar) wool
A crochet hook size 5.00
A wool needle for sewing in the ends

Measurement: 90 cm. long
                        6 cm. wide (at the widest part)

Tension: 5 d.c. = 3 cm.; 2 rows = 1 cm.

NOTE: The tie may be made longer or shorter as desired.

To make:

Begin with 11 ch.

1st row: 1 d.c. into 2nd ch. from hook, 1 d.c. into each ch. to end, 1 ch., turn (10 d.c.). **2nd to 30th rows:** 1 d.c. into each d.c. of last row, 1 ch., turn. **31st row:** 1 d.c. into first d.c., miss 1 d.c., 1 d.c. into next d.c., 1 d.c. into each of next 5 d.c., miss 1 d.c., 1 d.c. into last d.c., 1 ch., turn. (You have decreased 2 sts., and 8 d.c. now are left.) **32nd row:** 1 d.c. into each d.c., 1 ch., turn. **33rd to 51st rows:** Rep. 32nd row. **52nd row:** 1 d.c. into first d.c., miss 1 d.c., 1 d.c. into next d.c., 1 d.c. into each of next 3 d.c., miss 1 d.c., 1 d.c. into last d.c., 1 ch., turn. (You have decreased 2 more sts., and 6 d.c. now remain.) **53rd row:** 1 d.c. into each d.c., 1 ch., turn. **54th to 81st rows:** Rep. 53rd row. **82nd row:** 1 d.c. into first d.c., miss 1 d.c., 1 d.c. into next d.c., 1 d.c. into next d.c., miss 1 d.c., 1 d.c. into last d.c., 1 ch., turn. (You have decreased 2 more sts., and 4 d.c. now remain.) **83rd row:** 1 d.c. into each d.c., 1 ch., turn. **84th to 180th rows:** Rep. 83rd row, leaving out the 1 ch. at end of 180th row, break off the wool.

Fasten off ends neatly and firmly.

Treble (tr.) stitches

You have now had plenty of practice with double crochet stitches, and are ready to learn the treble stitch. Begin with 20 ch.

Hold the work exactly as you did for d.c. and remember that before you begin to make a treble stitch *the wool goes over the hook first*.

1.   Y.o.h., insert hook under the 2 top threads of *4th* ch. from hook (number 4 in Picture 1). The first 3 ch. will form the first stitch of the row, and the treble you are now going to make will count as the *second* stitch.

2.   Y.o.h., and draw through the 2 top threads just picked up (3 loops now on hook) (Picture 2).

3.   Y.o.h., and draw through the first 2 loops on hook (2 loops now on hook) (Picture 3).

4.   Y.o.h. again and draw through both loops on hook (1 loop is now left on hook). You have just made your first treble stitch (Picture 4).

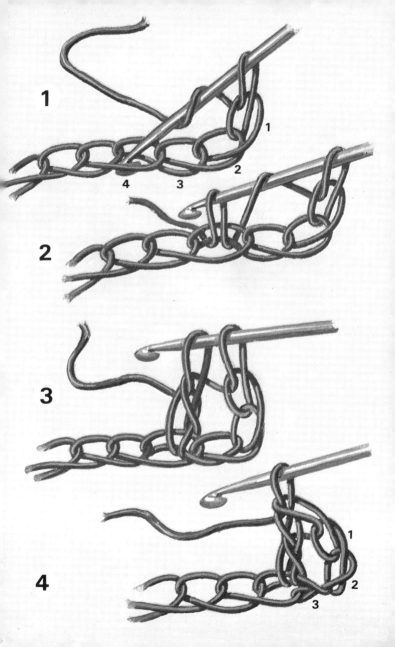

5. For the next treble stitch, y.o.h., insert hook under the 2 top threads of next chain, y.o.h., and draw through 2 threads, y.o.h. and draw through first 2 loops on hook, y.o.h. again and draw through last 2 loops on hook (1 loop now on hook and second treble made).

Repeat **5** to end of row, and then make 3 ch. and turn the work round (18 sts. in all) (Picture 5).

Next row: As before, the 3 turning ch. stand for the first stitch of this new row, y.o.h., insert hook under 2 top threads of next st. to the one at bottom of turning ch., y.o.h. and draw through both threads, y.o.h. and draw through first 2 loops on hook, y.o.h. and draw through last 2 loops on hook. (First tr. of new row made, which counts as 2nd stitch.)

Now work 1 tr. into each treble of previous row, making the last tr. into the top of the 3 turning ch. of previous row.

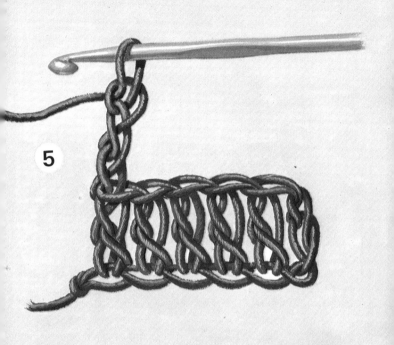

5

Practice: Keep working more and more rows over each
other until the movements are easy and all the stitches
evenly formed. Remember all the time to count 17 trs.
and 3 turning ch. as 18 sts. in each row.

Scarf

This scarf is made in rows of trebles. This matches the cap on page 36 and will give you some good practice.

3 20-gram balls double crêpe (or similar) wool

A crochet hook size 5.00

A wool needle for sewing in the ends

A piece of card 5 cm. deep, 15 cm. wide for fringes

Measurement: 80 cm. without fringe, by 15 cm.

Tension: 5 tr. = 3 cm.; 4 rows = 5 cm.

To make:

Begin with 27 ch.

1st row: 1 tr. into 4th ch. from hook, 1 tr. into every ch. to end (24 tr., with 3 turning ch. at beginning make 25 sts.), 3 ch., turn. **2nd row:** 1 tr. into stitch next to stitch at base of turning ch. just made, 1 tr. into every st. to the end, making the last tr. into top of turning ch. of previous row (25 sts.), 3 ch., turn. **3rd to 64th rows:** Rep. 2nd row, leaving out the 3 turning ch. at end of 64th row. Fasten off and sew in the ends.

Fringe: Wind yarn round card 78 times and cut along top edge. (Picture 1).

To fix the fringes, insert hook from back to front at one side of one end of scarf between 1st and 2nd trs., place the middle of 3 cut strands into hook (Picture 2), pull hook back through st. (Picture 3). Now fold all 6 ends of fringe over hook and draw them through loop on hook. Tighten the knot.

Knot similar fringes, leaving 2 tr. between each one, along both ends of scarf. Cut the ends even.

THE FRINGE

1

Cut

5cm.

15cm.

2

3

Cap to match the scarf

This cap goes well with the scarf on page 34 and will give you still more practice in the formation of trebles, helping you to make sure all the edges are even.

> *2 20-gram balls double crêpe (or similar) wool*
> *A crochet hook size 5.00*
> *10 strands for tassels as for scarf fringe*
> *A wool needle*

Measurement: To fit child 6 to 10 years
              Width round lower edge 45 cm.
              Depth 21 cm.

Tension: 5 tr. = 3 cm.; 4 rows = 5 cm.

To make:

Begin with 34 ch. and work 36 rows as for scarf. You will have 31 tr. and 3 turning ch. on every row, that is, 32 sts.

Fasten off and sew in all ends.

To make up:

Pin, and neatly oversew together the first and last rows for back seam.

Drawstring: Using 2 strands of yarn together, make 80 ch. and fasten off the ends.

Starting at centre front, thread drawstring between 6th and 7th trs. of every row, draw up and tie in a bow.

Using 5 strands each time, attach a tassel to each end of string as for scarf.

Half treble (hlf. tr.)

The next stitch to learn is the half treble. This is made in much the same way as the treble, except that the three loops on the hook, are all taken off at the same time.

Begin with 20 ch.

1. Y.o.h., insert hook under 2 top loops of 3rd ch. from hook, y.o.h., and draw this through loops just picked up (3 loops now on hook).

2. Y.o.h., and draw this through all 3 loops on hook (1 loop now on hook). You have just made your first half treble (Picture 2).

3. For the next hlf. tr., y.o.h., insert hook through 2 top loops of next ch., y.o.h., and draw this through loops just picked up (3 loops on hook).

4. Y.o.h., and draw this through all 3 loops on hook (1 loop on hook).

5. Repeat 3 and 4 to end of chain (18 hlf. tr. made, with 2 turning ch. make 19 sts.).

6. Make 2 ch., then turn work round.

7. Y.o.h., insert hook under 2 top loops of the stitch next to the one at the bottom of the 2 turning ch. just made.

8. Y.o.h., and draw through loops just picked up, y.o.h. again and draw through all 3 loops on hook.

Repeat 3 and 4 to end of row, making the last stitch by going into top of 2 turning ch. of previous row.

Practice: Keep making row upon row of hlf. tr. stitches until they are all evenly formed, and you can easily tell the difference between the hlf. trs. just practised and the d.c.s. and trs. you learned before.

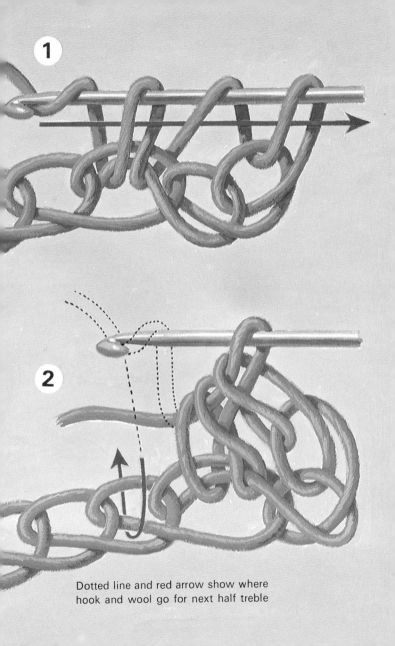

1

2

Dotted line and red arrow show where
hook and wool go for next half treble

Slip stitch (sl. st.)

As this is a very tiny stitch it is easier to learn if it is made over the top of a row of other stitches.

When you have finished practising the half trebles on page 38, do not break off the wool and you will then be able to work the slip stitches on top of these.

No turning chains are needed to make sl. sts. as they have hardly any height.

Turn the row of hlf. trs. round ready to make the slip stitches.

1. Insert hook under 2 top threads of the *first* stitch of the last row, y.o.h., and draw through all loops on hook (Picture 1) (1 sl. st. made).

2. For the next sl. st., insert hook under 2 top threads of next st., y.o.h., and draw through all loops on hook (Picture 2).

3. Keep making a sl. st. into each st. to end of row (19 sl. sts. made) (Picture 3).

NOTE: If you look closely at the row of sl. sts. just made, you will see only the row of top chain stitches at the top of the hlf. trs. of the previous row.

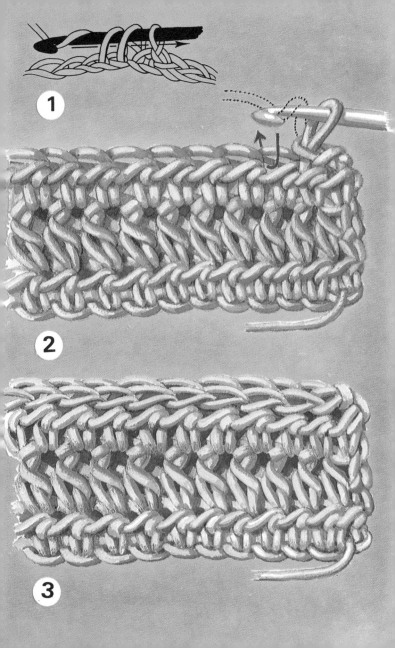

1

2

3

Belt

You will enjoy making this little belt and it will give you plenty of practice in making trs., hlf. trs. and sl. sts.

1 20-gram ball of double crêpe (or similar) wool
A crochet hook size 5.00
6 small shank buttons
A wool needle to link the buttons

Measurement: Width 7 cm., Length 50 cm.

Tension: 5 tr. = 3 cm.
         Rows 2, 3 and 4 together = 2.25 cm.

NOTE: The belt can be made in any length. Begin and end with a row of trs., as the links go through these.

To make:

Begin with 14 ch.

1st row: 1 tr. into 4th ch. from hook, 1 tr. in each ch. to end (11 tr., with turning ch. make 12 sts.), 2 ch., turn ready for the next row of hlf. trs.

2nd row: 1 hlf. tr. into st. next to base of turning ch., 1 hlf. tr. into every st. to end, making last st. into top of turning ch. of previous row. There will be no turning ch. as the next row will be sl. sts.

3rd row: 1 sl. st. into every st. of previous row (12 sl. sts.), 3 ch. to turn, ready for next row which will be trs.

4th row: 1 tr. into st. next to base of turning ch., 1 tr. into every st. to end (11 tr. with turning ch. make 12 sts.), 2 ch. to turn for next row of hlf. trs.

Repeat rows **2, 3** and **4** 21 times. Break off wool and fasten off neatly.

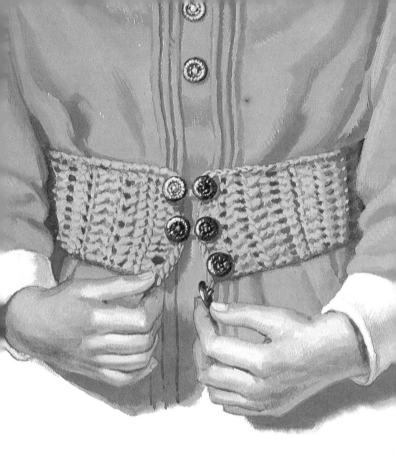

To make the links: Sew 2 buttons together, leaving about 1 cm. space between them, and fasten off securely. Repeat with the other 2 pairs of buttons.

To fasten the belt, push buttons through each end of belt to form links. When unfastening, only one side need be removed.

Rounds and squares – called 'motifs'

Many lovely things can be made by working in rounds, that is, instead of turning the work at the end of a row, you continue crocheting in an anti-clockwise direction (or clockwise if you are left-handed).

A motif which begins as a round can be turned into a square by the special formation of the stitches. Motifs can be used separately as little mats, or joined together to make anything from a jacket to a bedspread.

If you look closely at a motif, you will notice that on one side at the edges there is a row of top chain stitches facing you. This is the right side.

Working in rounds

Begin with 6 ch., join with a sl. st. to first ch. to make a ring (Pictures 1 and 2).

1st round: Make 8 d.c. into the ring (Picture 3), join with a sl. st. to first d.c. of round;

2nd round: Make 2 d.c. into the top chain stitch of every d.c. of the 1st round. This is an increase of 1 st. in each d.c. 16 d.c. now in the round (Picture 4).

NOTE: It is a good idea to mark the last stitch of the 1st round with a little gold safety pin, and to keep moving this to the last stitch of each round as it is made.

3rd round: *2 d.c. into next d.c., 1 d.c. into next d.c., rep. from * to end of round (24 d.c. now in the round).

Practice: Pull the work undone, and repeat above 3 rounds until the stitches flow easily and are evenly formed.

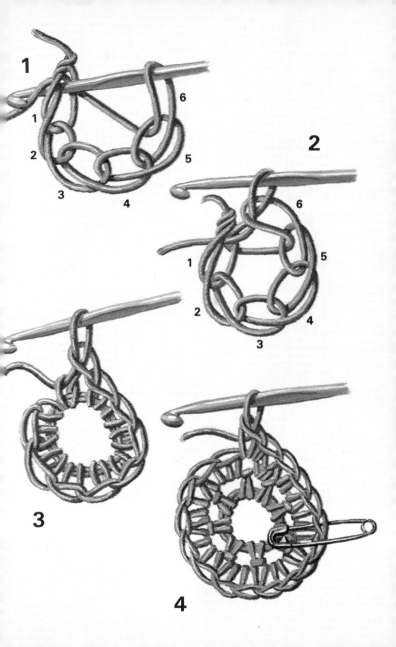

1

1

2

3

4

5

6

2

1

2

3

4

5

6

3

4

A little mat

This mat was made from an oddment of Twilley's *Knitcot*.

Measurement: 11.5 cm. across the widest part, which is called the *diameter*.

NOTE: During the first round you may find a little difficulty in getting all the 24 d.c. sts. into the ring. Keep pushing them back towards the beginning, and they will fit in very well.

To make:

Begin with 10 ch., and join with a sl. st. to first ch., to make a ring.

1st round: Make 24 d.c. into the ring, and join with 1 sl. st. to first d.c. of round. Slip the safety pin into the last d.c. of this round.

2nd round: 6 ch., * miss 1 d.c., 1 tr. into next d.c., 3 ch., rep. from * ending with 1 sl. st. into 3rd of 6 ch. (12 spaces). Move safety pin up to last st. of this round.

3rd round: Into each space work 1 d.c., 1 hlf. tr., 2 tr., 1 hlf. tr. and 1 d.c., making 1 sl. st. into first d.c. of round.

Move safety pin.

Fasten off and sew in ends neatly.

Making a square

This is very similar to working a round, except that as you progress, the shape becomes square.

A simple and attractive motif of this type, known as the Grannie Square, can be made in one, or more colours.

Oddments of double crêpe (or similar) wool
A crochet hook size 5.00
A wool needle

To make the Grannie Square

Begin with 8 ch., and join with a sl. st. into a ring.

1st round: 3 ch. (to count as 1 tr.), 2 tr. into ring (2 ch., 3 tr.) 3 times, 2 ch., 1 sl. st. into 3rd of 3 ch. at beginning of round, break off wool, and fasten off.

2nd round: With another colour, join wool to next 2 ch. space, 3 ch., 2 tr., 2 ch., 3 tr. all into the same space, 1 ch., * (3 tr., 2 ch., 3 tr.) in next 2 ch. space, 1 ch., rep. from * twice more, join to top of 3 ch. with 1 sl. st. Break off wool, as before.

3rd round: With another colour, join wool to next 2 ch. space, 3 ch., 2 tr., 2 ch., 3 tr. all into same space, * 1 ch., 3 tr., in next 1 ch. space, 1 ch., 3 tr., 2 ch., 3 tr. in next 2 ch. sp., rep. from * twice more, 1 ch., 3 tr. in 1 ch. sp., 1 ch., join with 1 sl. st., and fasten off wool.

4th round: With the first colour, join wool to next 2 ch. space, 3 ch., 2 tr., 2 ch., 3 tr. all into same space; now work 1 ch., 3 tr. into each 1 ch. space, and 1 ch., 3 tr., 2 ch., 3 tr. into each 2 ch. space, join with 1 sl. st., fasten off as before.

Sew each odd end neatly into its own colour.

Note: If a larger square is desired, just add more rounds, keeping the corners the same, and increasing the number of 1ch., 3tr., along each side by one in each round.

A poncho for dolly

A doll with shoulders about 7 cm. wide
Oddments of double crêpe (or similar) wool in 2 colours,
Light (L), and Dark (D)
A crochet hook size 5.00
Card measuring 4 cm. by 8 cm.

To make:

For every square use the **L** wool for the chain ring and 1st round, the outer border and neck edging; use the **D** wool for the 2nd round of each motif and the fringe.

Working only the first 2 rounds of the Grannie Square on page 48, make 8 motifs. Fasten off and sew in ends.

With right sides facing, pin one side of 2 motifs together and oversew together, taking one stitch from each motif. Join the motifs together as in drawing.

The outer border: With right side of poncho facing you, join the **L** wool into one corner space, and work as follows: 3 ch. for first tr., 2 tr., 1 ch., 3 tr. all into same 2 ch. space, 3 tr. into next 1 ch. space (3 tr. into two next 2 ch. spaces, 3 tr. into next 1 ch. space) twice, * 3 tr., 1 ch., 3 tr. all into corner 2 ch. space, 3 tr. into next 1 ch. space (3 tr. into next two 2 ch. spaces, 3 tr. into next 1 ch. space) twice, rep. from * twice more, join to top of 3 ch. with 1 sl. st. Fasten off and sew in the ends.

Neck: Join in **L**, 3 ch. into one corner, 1 tr. into every tr. and 1 tr. into every corner all round neck, join with 1 sl. st. to top of 3 ch.

Next round: 3 ch., 1 tr. into every tr., join with 1 sl. st. to top of 3 ch. Fasten off and sew in the ends.

Fringe: Wind **D** round card 112 times, cut, and knot 1 strand into every tr. and 1 strand into each corner.

1	2	3
8	SPACE FOR NECK	4
7	6	5

Each motif square measures 6.5 × 6.5 cm.
Poncho, without fringe, measures 21 cm. square.